W9-CJD-923

Friends of the
Houston Public Library

WILD CATS!
OF THE WORLD

JAGUARS
AND LEOPARDS

By Melissa Cole
Photographs by Tom and Pat Leeson

BLACKBIRCH PRESS

GALE GROUP
THOMSON LEARNING™

Detroit • New York • San Diego • San Francisco
Boston • New Haven, Conn. • Waterville, Maine
London • Munich

Published by Blackbirch Press
10911 Technology Place
San Diego, CA 92127

e-mail: customerservice@galegroup.com
Web site: www.galegroup.com/blackbirch

©2002 by Blackbirch Press
an imprint of the Gale Group
First Edition

All rights reserved. No part of this book may be reproduced in any form without permission in writing from Blackbirch Press, except by a reviewer.

Printed in China

10 9 8 7 6 5 4 3 2 1

Library of Congress Cataloging-in-Publication Data
Cole, Melissa
Jaguars and leopards / by Melissa Cole.
     p.   cm. — (Wild cats of the world)
Summary: Discusses the physical characteristics, feeding and mating behavior, and habitat of jaguars and leopards.
    ISBN 1-56711-447-4 (hardcover : alk. paper)
    1. Jaguar—Juvenile literature. 2. Leopard—Juvenile literature. [1.Jaguar. 2. Leopard.] I. Title. II. Series.
QL737.C23 C6424 2002
599.75′7—dc21
                                                   2001005315

Contents

Introduction

Leopards are found in Africa, the Middle East, and Asia.

Leopards are found in more areas of the world than any other big cat. These spotted wild cats are found in Africa, the Middle East, and southern Asia. Leopards can live in tropical forests, open grassland, deserts, mountains, and even cities. As long as there is water to drink, a variety of prey, and places to hide, leopards can survive.

The jaguar is a close cousin of the leopard. Scientists believe that thousands of years ago, these leopard-like cats traveled from Asia to the Americas. Jaguars live throughout much of South America, Central America, and Mexico. They once lived in Arizona, New Mexico, southern California, and Texas. Jaguar fossils have even been found as far north as the U.S.-Canadian border.

Today, it is rare to find any of these big cats north of Mexico. A jaguar's favorite habitat is dark, wet, tropical jungle. Yet, jaguars also have been found living in the deserts of Mexico as well as high in the mountains of Peru and Bolivia.

Jaguars are found in South America, Central America, and Mexico.

5

Jaguar or Leopard?

Jaguars and leopards look so much alike it is difficult to tell them apart. Jaguars, however, are usually bigger than leopards. They have thick muscular bodies; broad heads; short, stocky legs; and large paws. A jaguar's spots form circular rings with a dot in the center. These patterns are called rosettes.

Leopards are the smallest of the big cats.

Leopard spots are smaller, and they don't have a dot in the middle.

Jaguars are the third-largest cats in the world. Only lions and tigers are bigger. Male jaguars weigh between 120 and 200 pounds (54 and 91 kg), while females usually weigh between 80 and 100 pounds (36 and 45 kg). Their bodies can grow to more than 7 feet (2 m) from nose to tail.

Leopards are the smallest members of the "great cat" family—cats that roar and do not purr. Leopards can weigh between 65 and 180 pounds (29 and 82 kg). They range in length from 5 to 7 feet (1.5 to 2 m). Males are usually twice as large as females.

Both jaguars and leopards have cubs that appear black at birth. Instead of the yellow fur of adults, they have blackish-brown fur with black spots.

The golden spotted coats of adult jaguars and leopards help them blend with their surroundings. When sun shines through grass or leaves, it creates a speckled pattern of dark and light that is similar to the pattern on the coats of the big cats. This helps the cats hide from both predators and prey.

Young leopards have blackish fur.

Leopards and jaguars have long whiskers that allow them to sense their way as they prowl about in the dark. Soft paw pads and fur between their toes help them walk softly on dry twigs and leaves. They can pull their deadly claws into special pockets in their paws to keep them sharp.

The tails of both jaguars and leopards are long and thick, which helps them balance when they pounce on prey. These handy tails are white underneath, which helps tiny cubs follow their mothers through thick underbrush.

Jaguars have larger spots than leopards.

Special Features

Both leopards and jaguars eat mostly meat. They have long, pointed canine teeth that help them grasp and kill their prey. Their back teeth slice their food into bite-sized pieces. Their rough tongues, which are covered with tiny hooks called papillae, are perfect for cleaning the last bits of meat off the bone. These useful tongues also clean up fur and faces after a meal.

Like other cats, leopards and jaguars have excellent vision. Their pupils can grow small to keep out bright sun or expand to let in extra light for night-time hunting. They also have extremely sensitive hearing. This helps them listen to prey without being noticed.

Long, pointed canine teeth are perfect for grasping and killing prey.

By listening to the prey's movements, a leopard or jaguar can pinpoint its location and creep silently toward it. The sense of smell is not as important as sight and hearing when it comes to hunting. Leopards and jaguars mostly use their sense of smell to tell if other animals have entered their territories.

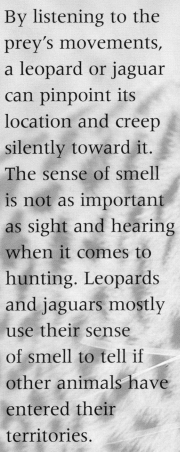

Leopards have excellent eyesight in light or dark.

Social Life

A leopard growls a warning.

Jaguars and leopards spend most of their time alone. Males and females spend time together only when they mate. Both leopards and jaguars stake out territories—areas where they regularly search for food, water, and places to rest. The size of a territory or home range depends on the supply of prey.

Female jaguars raise their cubs within a home range that is usually 10 to 15 square miles (16 to 24 sq km), while males have territories twice that size. Jaguars often have smaller territories during rainy times of year when land is flooded.

Female territories often overlap. Males, however, try to avoid other males, and their territories do not cross over. Leopards and jaguars rarely fight with their own species. They stay away from one another and find mates by communicating from a distance.

These big cats use body language to show their mood. If they are in danger, for example, their ears flatten against their heads and their tails lash back and forth. They often flatten themselves against the ground or back away slowly. When males and females are curious or friendly, they lift their tails and ears. Sometimes they rub necks and lick each other.

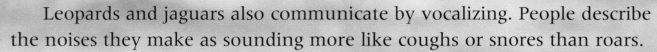

Leopards and jaguars also communicate by vocalizing. People describe the noises they make as sounding more like coughs or snores than roars.

Big cats mark their territories by scratching trees with their sharp claws. Cats have many scent glands around the mouth, cheeks and chin, between the toes, and at the base of the tail. When leopards and jaguars scratch trees, they leave behind a scent as well as the marks. They also leave droppings and spray urine on rocks, bushes, and clumps of grass that border their territory. Other animals who smell the scent marks know they are trespassing and that intruding may be dangerous.

Leopards sometimes communicate by rubbing necks.

Expert Hunters

Although jaguars and leopards have many similar behaviors, their hunting methods are quite different. Leopards sometimes hunt during the day, though they are mainly nocturnal and so hunt at night. While hunting, they slink with their bellies close to the ground. When they close in on their prey, they pounce, often leaping 20 feet (6.1 m) in a single bound! A leopard may also drop down from a tree branch onto prey passing below.

A leopard strangles its prey by grabbing it at the throat. Sometimes it will cut the spinal cord with a bite to the back of the neck. If the animal is too big to eat all at once, a leopard will come back day after day until nothing is left. Leopards are strong enough to carry prey twice their size up into a tree— out of reach of lions and wild dogs.

A leopard carries a mongoose to a safe place before feeding.

Leopards are not picky eaters. They prefer to eat larger animals such as impalas, gazelles, and wildebeests. However, they also hunt frogs, lizards, birds, monkeys, rats, pigs, and baboons. They add to their diet with grass, eggs, fruit, and meat they steal from lions and hyenas. Sometimes they even lie on the banks of rivers and lakes and pull fish out of the water with their paws!

Jaguars live in a different habitat, so they prey on different animals than leopards do. Like leopards, however, jaguars also snake along the ground and ambush their prey at night. The animals that jaguars hunt change throughout the year. Some foods, such as turtle or iguana eggs, are available only during a certain season. Jaguars eat sea turtles during nesting season when the turtles come onto beaches to lay their eggs.

Jaguars also hunt large animals such as pig-like tapirs, which they bury and eat later. Unlike most cats, they do not seem to mind eating rotten meat. Jaguars also kill turkeys, armadillos, and capybaras—the world's largest rodents. They also climb trees in search of birds, sloths, and monkeys. They jump right into bodies of water, searching for fish, river otters, snakes, and caiman, which are small alligator-like animals.

Jaguars have the most powerful jaws of any cat. They are the only cats that kill by biting through their victim's skull. They also knock prey down with a slap of their large paws, which can break an animal's neck. Once they have killed their prey, jaguars often drag the carcass a long way to a quiet area to feed. Sometimes they even drag their meal up into a tree.

Leopards and jaguars often climb into trees to feed or hide.

The Mating Game

Male and female leopards get together only to mate.

For most of the year, leopards and jaguars live alone. Males and females get together only to mate, then they separate again within a few days. Leopard mating can take place at any time during the year, and cubs can be born in any season. Jaguars often mate between March and September. Thus, the cubs are born between June and December when it is not too rainy in the forest.

Females attract males by vocalizing and by spraying urine on bushes, rocks, and trees. Males are attracted by chemicals in the female's scent mark. They know that she is ready to mate. Both jaguars and leopards are secretive and avoid people. Therefore, scientists do not know much about their mating behavior. Female leopards and jaguars usually raise cubs on their own, without help from the father.

Raising Young

Jaguars and leopards raise their cubs in similar ways. Their pregnancies last between three and four months. During this time they continue to hunt. They search for a hiding place, or den, where they can safely give birth to their litters. This den is usually a quiet shelter of low bushes, or a rocky cave.

Jaguars give birth to between one and four cubs per litter. Leopards usually give birth to two to three babies at a time, though they can have as many as six cubs in a litter.

An African leopard cub, about three months old.

Cubs weigh 2 to 3 pounds (1 to 1.4 kg) when they are born and are completely helpless. Their eyes are sealed shut, and they cannot hear or even crawl. Their mothers stay with them for two or three days without leaving to hunt. She licks them with her rough tongue to increase their blood circulation. She nurses them almost constantly. In order to continue producing milk, both jaguar and leopard mothers need to feed themselves. So, after a few days they leave for short periods of time to hunt.

This period is dangerous for the cubs. Hungry predators are often nearby. Careful mothers may move their cubs from one den to another to trick predators.

After 10 days, the cubs usually open their bluish eyes for the first time. Soon their eyes become a golden, amber color like those of their parents. At three weeks, the young cubs are able to walk on steady paws. They still stay quietly inside their den, especially if their mother has gone hunting.

At two to three months of age, the cubs begin to follow their mother on hunting expeditions. Cubs often practice hunting by sneaking up on each other.

An Amur leopard in Asia.

Most cubs are protected by their mothers until they are old enough to hunt on their own.

They roll and tumble, pouncing on each other and even chomping down with sharp little teeth! These games help them grow strong and gain the coordination they will need to hunt.

Later, cubs begin to hunt small animals. Even though they are still feeding on their mother's rich milk, they also eat meat. Sometimes their mother will bring them a small animal such as a baby deer or antelope that she has caught but not killed. Then she has the cubs practice stalking, pouncing on and killing the prey. It can take almost two years before the youngsters are ready to hunt on their own.

At two years old, female jaguars and leopards are ready to mate. Young male cubs set out to establish their own territories, while females often take over part of their mother's home range. Soon the female youngsters will have cubs of their own.

Jaguars live to be about 11 to 18 years old in the wild. They can live more than 25 years in captivity. Leopards live for about 12 years. They may live as long as 23 years in zoos.

Jaguars, Leopards, and Humans

Leopards can adapt to almost any environment. Unfortunately, people are using leopard territories, such as forests and grasslands, to build farms, roads, towns, and golf courses. Leopards are sometimes forced to live near humans, where they end up preying on livestock because their natural prey is gone.

Leopards are sometimes forced to live near humans.

Some countries have set aside land for wildlife parks. Others, however, think of leopards as pests. In these places, people shoot and poison leopards to get rid of them. There are also still poachers who kill these animals for their beautiful skin,

Many jaguars have been hunted illegally.

sharp claws, and teeth. Some types of leopard—such as the Anatolian leopard, which lives in Turkey, Syria, and Lebanon—are almost extinct. Zoos are trying to breed these leopards in captivity.

Jaguars rarely attack people and are protected in most countries that have jaguar populations. Still, thousands of these big cats are illegally hunted for their fur, claws, teeth, and other parts.

Today, the biggest threat to jaguars is not hunting, but the loss of their land. As the human population grows, more land on which to live must be cleared. This destroys the rain forest and forces jaguars to live on smaller areas of land. Jaguars have difficulty hunting and mating when they are isolated in small pockets of forest.

A rare snow leopard.

It is rare to see leopards and jaguars in the wild because they fear humans and because their fur blends in so well with their surroundings. Scientists are trying to study jaguars in the wild by photographing them with remote cameras and putting radio-tracking collars around their necks.

The country of Belize in Central America has a large park called Cockscomb Basin Jaguar Preserve. Here, jaguars are protected and visitors come to catch a glimpse of these great cats. Animal lovers say other countries should follow Belize in setting aside land in which jaguars, leopards, and other wild animals can live freely.

Glossary

ambush To hide and then attack.

den The home of a wild animal.

habitat The place and natural conditions in which a plant or an animal lives.

litter A group of cats born at the same time to one mother.

nocturnal An animal that is active at night.

prey An animal that is hunted by another animal for food.

prowl To move around quietly and secretly.

Further Reading

Books

Jordan, Bill. *Leopard: Habitats, Life Cycles, Food Chains* (Natural World). TX: Raintree Steck-Vaughn Publishers, 2002.

Malaspina, Ann. *The Jaguar* (Endangered Animals and Habitats). San Diego, CA: Lucent Books, 2000.

Middleton, Don. *Big Cats, Jaguars.* NY: The Rosen Publishing Group, 1999.

Watt, Melanie. *Jaguars.* TX: Raintree Steck-Vaughn Publishers, 1998.

Web Sites

The Cyber Zoomobile, Leopards and Jaguars—*http://www.primenet.com/~brendel/*

Defenders of Wildlife—*http://www.defenders.org/wildlife/new/bigcats/jag.html*

Index

HACRX   +
         599
         .755
         C

COLE, MELISSA S.
    JAGUARS AND LEOPARDS

ACRES HOME
04/06